Mel Bay Presents

SIGHT READING
for the CONTEMPORARY GUITARIST

GW00566927

by TOM BRUNER

1 2 3 4 5 6 7 8 9 0

Visit us on the Web at www.melbay.com — E-mail us at email@melbay.com

Tom Bruner...

As a guitarist, composer, arranger, and conductor of music, Tom has many years of experience in the music and entertainment production fields, while working with every conceivable style and genre of music performance. Some of the many facets of Tom's musical career are highlighted below.

• Musical Director (arranger, conductor, and music producer) on over 60 television shows (including the Golden Globe Awards – for 12 years, and the Academy Of Country Music Awards – for 18 years).
• Has arranged and conducted music for many of the brightest stars in the entertainment business.
• Performed as a studio musician/guitarist on countless television productions, movies, records and jingles.
• Nominated for a Grammy Award in 1998 for arranging and conducting the BMG CD release, Secret Love for singer Lori Morgan.
• Arranged and produced the performance tracks for the production of A Chorus Line at the Reno Hilton.
• Is listed in Who's Who In Entertainment, Who's Who In America and Who's Who In The World.

Television Show Musical Director

Tom has served as Musical Director (arranger/conductor) on over 60 television shows, including:

• The Golden Globe Awards (for 12 years)
• The Academy of Country Music Awards (for 18 years)
• The Olympic Flag Jam (a super-show produced by Dick Clark at the Atlanta Dome in 1992, celebrating the hosting of the 94 Olympics)
• The 1st, 2nd, 3rd & 4th Black Gold Awards (w/Lou Rawls)
• The Great American Sing Along (w/Steve Allen)
• The Lou Rawls Parade of Stars (for 3 years)
• Ray Charles 40th Anniversary Salute
• I Love Men (w/Donna Mills)
• The 1st & 2nd US Magazine Awards
• TV Round The World (HBO)
• Sea World Special All Star Lone Star Celebration (w/Marie Osmond & Natalie Cole)
• The NBA Awards
• Slapstick Studio (w/Dick Shawn)
• Thanks For Caring (telethon for C.A.R.E. w/Gloria Loring)
• Celebrity Fun Cruise (w/Englebert Humberdinck & Andy Gibb)

PREFACE

Up until a few years ago. finding a guitar player who could sight read melodic lines was about as rare as a whooping crane. But today. because of wide spread study and the use and popularity of the guitar. melodic sight reading has become a very necessary part of guitar playing. Composers and arrangers are no longer "afraid" to write complex melodic parts for guitar. It is now important for a working guitar player to be as proficient a sight reader as any brass or woodwind player. Thus. the reason for my writing this book.

It is my assumption that the student of this study already knows the basics of reading music; i.e. knowing the name of notes on the staff. simple rhythmic counting, etc. While extremely complex rhythms have been avoided so as not to overshadow problems of melodic interval execution. basic rhythms and time signature counting problems are presented. But my main concern in writing this book is to have the student instinctively know the guitar neck inside and out and be able to execute any melody at sight. no matter what problems it may present in its interval relationships. For that reason. most of the exercises will not be made up of *memorable* melodies or phrases. It is essential that a student of sight reading not play an exercise *by ear.* after having learned it. I hope it will be almost impossible for a student to learn these exercises by ear. He must *read* each and every note and overcome each and every problem in a melodic execution if he is to develop his abilities as a sight reader.

Remember. the melodies and exercises in this book may sound extremely discordant in relation to those you might normally play. They were written that way specifically to teach you how to read and overcome unexpected problems at sight. They must be played with a great deal of concentration and looked upon as one challenge after another. You will soon find it to be very exciting meeting and overcoming each challenge. This hopefully will give you the same kind of satisfaction as any other kind of "difficult" playing which "challenges" you into eventual mastery. Each challenge, from etude to etude, line to line. phrase to phrase and note to note—when met--will strenghten your ability as a sight reader. And with this ability intact. your position in the world of music will be so much more secure!

I wish the student good luck in using this book. I can assure you if you use it and study it as it was designed. you will be able to sight read on the guitar just about as well as you will ever need to! And by developing this sight reading ability. you will insure your success as a professional or semi-professional guitarist.

TABLE OF CONTENTS

LINEAR SIGHT READING ON THE GUITAR

Sight reading on any instrument is never an easy task. But it is a skill which can be learned, through drill and practice, just as any other *visual-motor-response* can be learned, whether it be typing, key punch operator, or short wave radio morse code. Sight reading on any musical instrument involves:

1. Recognizing written instructions (notation).
2. Deciphering and interpreting those instructions in your brain.
3. Sending out the proper instructions from your brain to your fingers, thus enabling you to perform those instructions.

All of these three processes must be done instantaneously in sight reading. In addition to these *physical processes*, a musician must also *interpret musically* these written instructions in order to play with an expressive, sensitive musical performance. In other words, much of the sight reading process is *recognition and response*—being a robot, a computer, a Pavlovian dog if you will. But more importantly, sight reading involves creative *musical interpretation*—injecting your own heart and soul into the sight reading performance—something a robot or a computer or a Pavlovian dog *cannot do*.

Sight reading on the guitar can be seemingly an insurmountable problem because of the very nature of the guitar neck configuration. Look at these examples. I have chosen five notes, all of which can be played in several places. Look at diagram Ⓒ in each of the examples to see the *written note*. Diagram Ⓑ shows you the different places on the neck where that particular note can be played. Diagram Ⓐ corresponds directly to diagram Ⓑ, fret for fret and shows you exactly where every note which could possibly be written for the guitar would lie. It is *very important* that you look at each of these examples and begin to understand, in diagram form, where notes lie on the guitar and how *most all notes* (except for low A♭ down to low E) can be played in at least two and as many as five or six places!

FINGERBOARD REFERENCE CHART

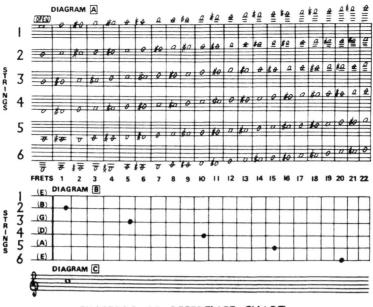

FINGERBOARD REFERENCE CHART

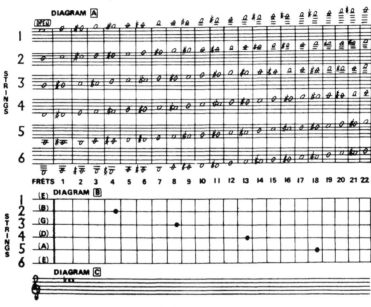

FINGERBOARD REFERENCE CHART

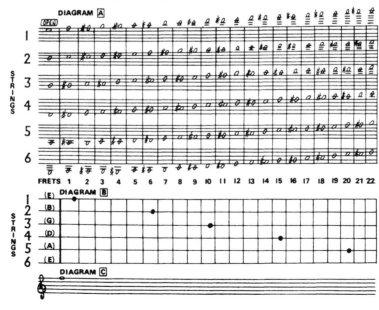

FINGERBOARD REFERENCE CHART

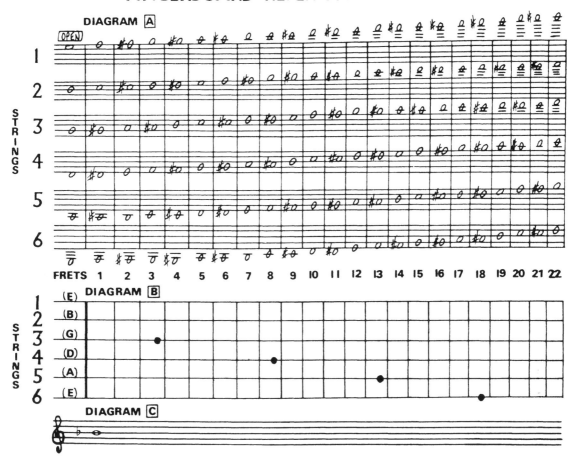

FINGERBOARD REFERENCE CHART

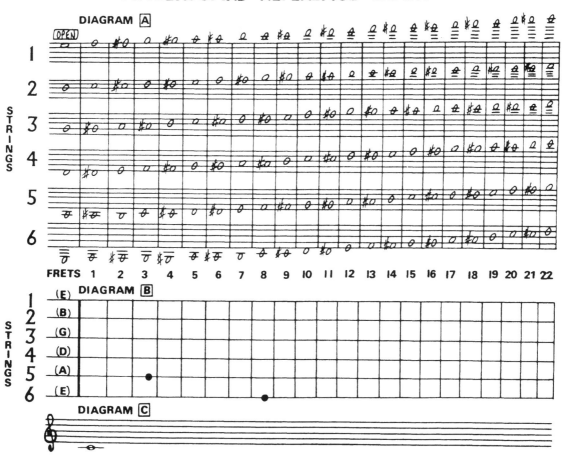

SIGHT READ BY REGIONS ON THE GUITAR

When sight reading, always read by register. In other words, see what the highest and lowest notes in a given passage are and read in that region of the guitar neck. It is very important you understand that when you are literally sight reading music for the first time, the first obligation you have to both yourself and the ensemble in which you are playing is to get the notes out. This does not always happen via the most preferable guitaristic fingering. Of course, on occasion, you may glance at a four-bar passage you are to play and immediately see a melodic pattern which you can relate to a scale position fingering pattern on the neck. And this is all well and good.

But when you are into a heavy sight reading situation where you have pages and pages of notes and there is absolutley no time to map out preferable guitar position fingerings, the only alternative you have is to look quickly to see what the highest and lowest notes are, at least for a half a page or so, and go to that region of the neck, simply playing the

notes as you see them. You have to instinctively know that if you see this note and you are in the middle region of the guitar neck, this note is played on the third string, fifth fret. You recognize the note - you play the note. If you happen to be able to play it with the first finger - great! Or if you happen to play it with the third finger, that's great too! The main thing is that you recognize the note and immediately go to that note and play it. The place you go to play the note will depend on which part of the guitar neck your left hand is in. What determines where your left hand is located is the register (lowest to highest note) where the melody lies. This is in the principle of reading by register and regions on the guitar.

I should make a point at this time something which is very important to studying my sight reading approach. I'm not concerning myself with teaching guitar techniques in this book. I'm not teaching scale and arpeggio exercises. I am only teaching sight reading. I assume that the student has studied, and practices diligently, scale and fingering exercises. This is an absolute prerequisite to being able to begin to come to grips with the problem of sight reading. If the student instinctively knows and diligently practices scales, arpeggios, and related fingering exercises on the guitar neck, then fingering problems which occur during sight reading will naturally take care of themselves. In other words, what my method books on sight reading will attempt to do is to get you to break away from the blinders of guitar positions as a method of sight reading. I want you to see a note, recognize what that note is, know where it is located in the region of the neck in which you are located, and play the note. If you can do this - see the note and immediately know where it is on the neck and not consciously concern yourself with guitar positions or guitaristic scale fingerings, then guitar "fingering" problems will subconsciously take care of themselves.

For this reason - to break you away from sight reading by consciously relating everything you read to a scale or guitar position fingering, none of the exercises in any of my sight reading books or studies will be written with a key signature.

One final point on this technique of sight reading must be made. Reading by register is no deep dark secret that I've dicovered. Almost all of the great sight readers on the guitar, which I've had the pleasure of knowing, read by this method. And once again, I must reiterate the vital importance of knowing and spontaneously using guitar position and guitar scale fingerings. You will automatically be playing and using these as you read through the various regions of the guitar neck. And after the requirement of the first reading of a piece of music has been completed - when you have the time to look at a particular passage which you have to read - you will surely work out or map out the most preferable guitaristic fingerings. But initially you should only concern yourself with getting as many of the notes as possible. This is the bottom line in sight reading - having to look at something for the first time with no time for preparation and immediately, on the spot, come up with the notes and perform them in a musical manner.

REGION I

Region 1 on the guitar would be notes lying in a register from low E to Bb above the staff. This region on the guitar neck would look like this on our diagram.

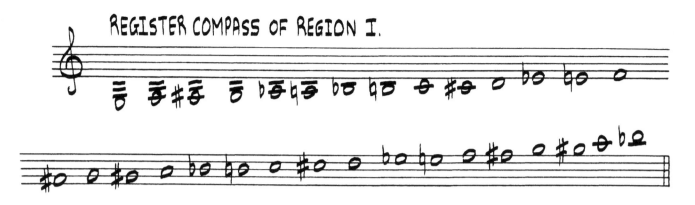

REGISTER COMPASS OF REGION I.

FINGERBOARD REFERENCE CHART

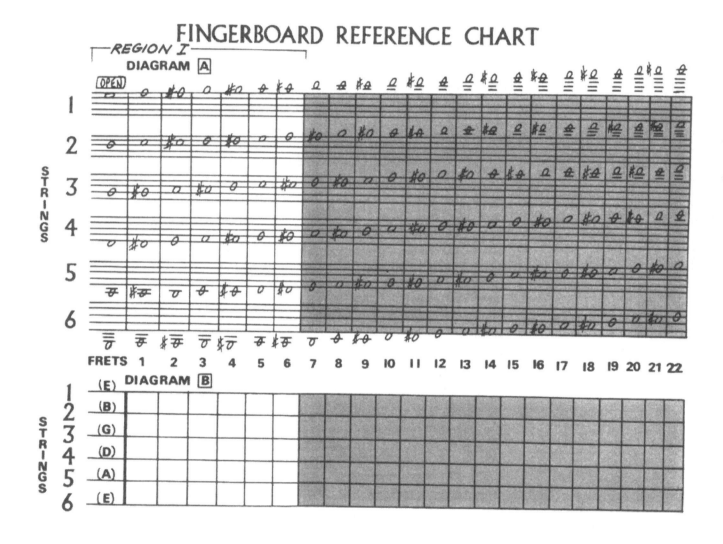

If you will now lay the four fingers of your left hand over this region of the guitar neck, you will see that your fingers will lie in a relative position to playing *any* of the notes in this register (low E to Bb above the staff).

THE RECOGNITION OF NOTES AND PLAYING
OF MELODIC INTERVALS IN REGION 1

The following exercises have been written in the simplest possible rhythms as an exercise for you to become familiar with notes in Region 1. *Again, there are no key signatures written in any of these exercises and all accidentals are canceled at the new bar line.*

The first few exercises are designed to teach you the various notes on the individual strings. After you feel comfortable playing these exercises, then go on to the exercises which deal with the entire scope of Region 1. Remember, *always practice the exercises in the book using a metronome.* If the metronome marking is too fast, put the metronome setting to a slow, comfortable tempo, gradually increasing the tempo as your reading proficiency increases. But remember—*always play strictly in a tempo and do not stop if you stumble over certain notes—always keep pace with whatever tempo you start out with!* If that particular tempo is too fast, then set the metronome at a slower tempo. It doesn't matter how slow the tempo is *as long as you adhere to a tempo!* This is the most basic principle of learning how to sight read.

ETUDE 1
PLAY THIS EXERCISE ON THE FIRST THREE STRINGS OF REGION I

PLAY THIS EXERCISE ON THE BOTTOM THREE STRINGS OF REGION I

PLAY THIS EXERCISE ON THE FIRST THREE STRINGS OF REGION I

PLAY THIS EXERCISE ON THE BOTTOM THREE STRINGS OF REGION I

PLAY THIS EXERCISE ENTIRELY IN REGION I

PLAY THIS EXERCISE ENTIRELY IN REGION I

PLAY THIS EXERCISE ENTIRELY IN REGION I

21

ETUDE 8

PLAY THIS EXERCISE ENTIRELY IN REGION I

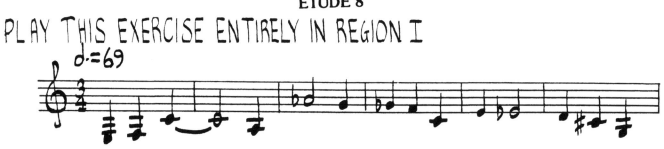

23

ETUDE 9
PLAY THIS EXERCISE ENTIRELY IN REGION I

PLAY THIS EXERCISE ENTIRELY IN REGION I

PLAY THIS EXERCISE ENTIRELY IN REGION I

PLAY THIS EXERCISE ENTIRELY IN REGION I

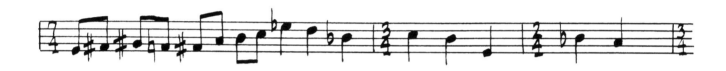

PLAY THIS EXERCISE ENTIRELY IN REGION I

REGION II

Region II on the guitar neck would encompass notes lying in a register from low G to high D.

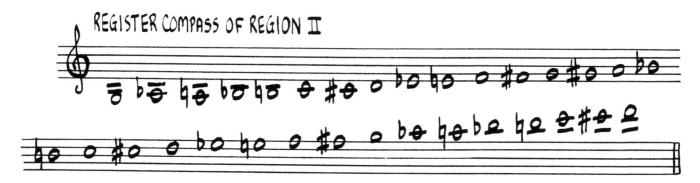

REGISTER COMPASS OF REGION II

This region would look like this on our guitar neck diagram.

FINGERBOARD REFERENCE CHART

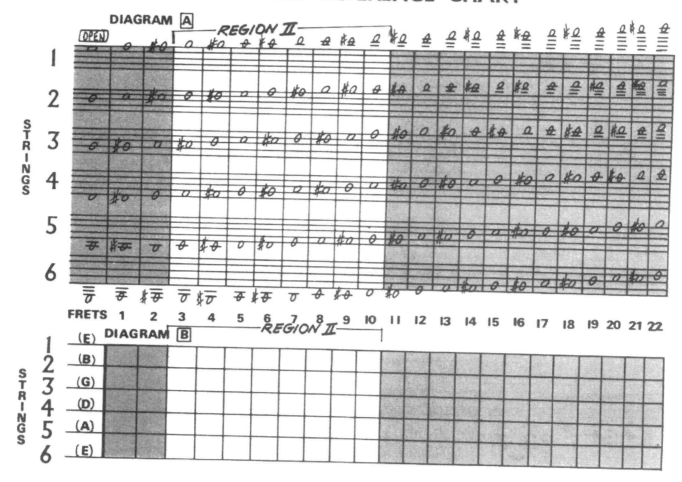

By laying the left hand over this region and using the thumb as a pivot, the entire compass of the register of the region can easily by played.

Play all the exercises for Region II strictly in tempo *with a metronome*. The metronome markings are optimum for the advanced sight reader. I suggest setting the tempo *slowly*, in a comfortable speed. It doesn't matter if the metronome is in a very slow tempo at first, *as long as a tempo is adhered to*.

PLAY THIS EXERCISE ON THE FIRST THREE STRINGS OF REGION II

PLAY THIS EXERCISE ON THE BOTTOM THREE STRINGS OF REGION II

PLAY THIS EXERCISE ON THE FIRST THREE STRINGS OF REGION II

PLAY THIS EXERCISE ON THE BOTTOM THREE STRINGS OF REGION II

ETUDE 18

PLAY THIS EXERCISE ON THE FIRST THREE STRINGS OF REGION II

PLAY THIS EXERCISE ENTIRELY IN REGION II

ETUDE 20

PLAY THIS EXERCISE ENTIRELY IN REGION II

43

PLAY THIS EXERCISE ENTIRELY IN REGION II

PLAY THIS EXERCISE ENTIRELY IN REGION II

PLAY THIS EXERCISE ENTIRELY IN REGION II

47

PLAY THIS EXERCISE ENTIRELY IN REGION II

REGION III

Region III on the guitar neck would encompass notes lying in a register from low B♭ to high G.

REGISTER COMPASS OF REGION III

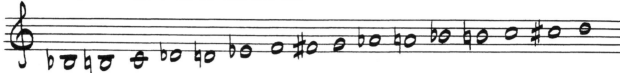

This region would look like this on our guitar neck diagram.

FINGERBOARD REFERENCE CHART

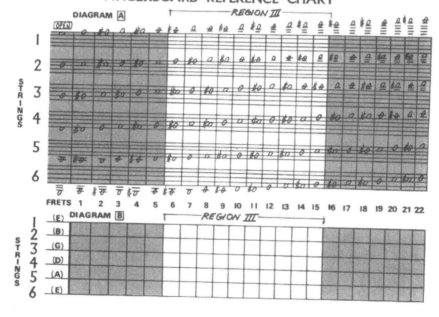

When playing these exercises, always adhere to a strict tempo. Set the metronome slow at first and gradually increase the speed. If you stumble over notes or even miss notes, *keep going*. Treat these exercises as if you were performing them as a member of an ensemble, thus staying up with the tempo you set. Remember, if you are really sight reading in an ensemble and you stumble over notes, you have to keep going. The conductor will not stop the tempo of the piece of music for you to "catch up". **50**

PLAY THIS EXERCISE ON THE 1ST THREE STRINGS IN REGION III

PLAY THIS EXERCISE ON THE BOTTOM THREE STRINGS IN REGION Ⅲ

PLAY THIS EXERCISE ON THE TOP THREE STRINGS IN REGION III

PLAY THIS EXERCISE ON THE BOTTOM THREE STRINGS IN REGION III

PLAY THIS EXERCISE ON TOP THREE STRINGS IN REGION III

PLAY THIS EXERCISE ON BOTTOM THREE STRINGS IN REGION III

PLAY THIS EXERCISE ENTIRELY IN REGION III

PLAY THIS EXERCISE ENTIRELY IN REGION III

PLAY THIS EXERCISE ENTIRELY IN REGION III

PLAY THIS EXERCISE ENTIRELY IN REGION III

PLAY THIS EXERCISE ENTIRELY IN REGION III

PLAY THIS EXERCISE ENTIRELY IN REGION III

PLAY THIS EXERCISE ENTIRELY IN REGION III

♩=144

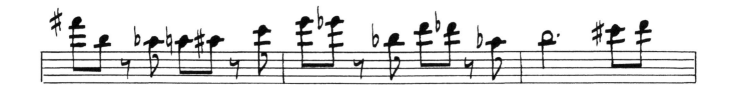

65

PLAY THIS EXERCISE ENTIRELY IN REGION III

REGION IV

Region IV on the guitar neck would encompass notes lying in a register from E on the bottom of the staff to high C.

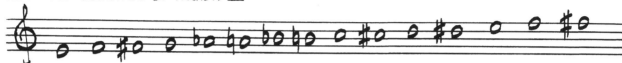

This region would look like this on our guitar neck diagram.

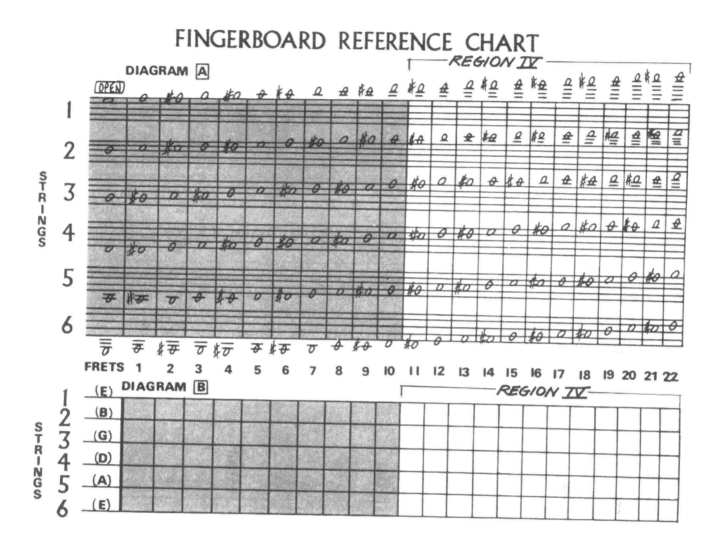

FINGERBOARD REFERENCE CHART

Region IV on the guitar is the stratosphere in terms of register. It is vital that you have a good facility for reading in this range of notes with its multiple ledger lines and "close together" frets. Many times composers and arrangers will write parts for you in this register which, unless you have this facility, you may find to be very difficult. Learning to read all the ledger lines is no different in principle from sight reading in any other register. You must *recognize, decipher, and react*.

When playing extended passages using notes in the extreme register, do not shift down to a lower range. You must learn to stay up in this high region for the notes which come back down inside the staff in order to "grab" the high notes.

Again, I emphasize—*play these exercises in a strict tempo, no matter how slow at first!* After your facility in this region is proficient, an additional exercise would be to play some exercises from Region I up an octave. This would help develop your ability to read passages written in one place, but playing them in another. It is *very common* that guitarists are asked to play written passages up an octave from where they are actually written (or down an octave from where they are written).

69

PLAY THIS EXERCISE ON THE FIRST THREE STRINGS IN REGION Ⅳ

PLAY THIS EXERCISE ON THE BOTTOM THREE STRINGS IN REGION Ⅳ

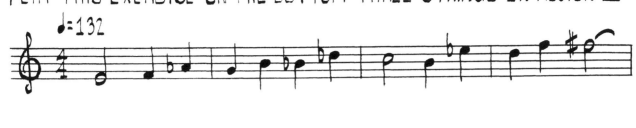

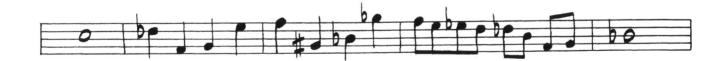

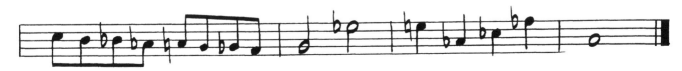

ETUDE 41

PLAY THIS EXERCISE ON THE 1ST THREE STRINGS IN REGION IV.

PLAY THIS EXERCISE ON THE BOTTOM THREE STRINGS IN REGION Ⅳ

PLAY THIS EXERCISE ENTIRELY IN REGION IV

PLAY THIS EXERCISE ENTIRELY IN REGION IV

PLAY THIS EXERCISE ENTIRELY IN REGION Ⅳ

PLAY THIS EXERCISE ENTIRELY IN REGION IV

Once you have practiced and mastered Region IV, then go back everday and read through *all* the exercises in this book. *Then* buy as many stacks of music literature written for other instruments as possible and sight read through them daily. Clarinet, flute, violin, oboe, and xylophone literature is especially good. Modern jazz saxophone and trumpet etudes also are very helpful. But the main thing you must do to build and maintain an ability to sight read linear passages on the guitar is *read, read, read, read!!*

Printed in Great Britain
by Amazon